Freaky Faces

David and Patricia Armentrout

Rourke
Publishing LLC
Vero Beach, Florida 32964

www.rourkepublishing.com

PHOTO CREDITS: © Eric Isselée: Cover © Holger W.: Title Page; © Nancy Nehring: page 4; © Dr. Morley Read: page 5; © Jim Mills: page 6; © Snowleopard1: page 7; © Scott Winegarden: page 8; © Shootov Igor: page 9; © Heather L. Jones: page 10; © Lynsey Allan: page 11; © Jeya: page 12; © Sergey Popov V: page 13, © Ariel Bravy: page 14; © Ryhor M Zasinets: page 15; © Niranjan: page 16; © Don Long: page 17; © Wong Kok Choy: page 18; ©N Joy Neish: page 19 top; © Joe Gough: page 19 bottom; © Kitch Bain: page 20; © Ferenc Cegledi: page 21; © Dr. Morley Read: page 22; © Cathy Keifer: page 23; © aaah: page 24; © Tomasz Pietryszek, © Ryan Morgan: page 25, © Gail Johnson: page 26; © Four Oaks page 27 top, 29; © Roger Devenish Jones: page 27 bottom; © EcoPrint: page 28; © Morley Read: page 30

Editor: Kelli Hicks

Cover Design: Nicola Stratford: bdpublishing.com

Page Design: Renee Brady

Library of Congress Cataloging-in-Publication Data

Armentrout, David, 1962-
 Freaky faces / David and Patricia Armentrout.
   p. cm. -- (Weird and wonderful animals)
 ISBN 978-1-60472-303-8 (hardcover)
 ISBN 978-1-60472-800-2 (softcover)
 1. Animals--Miscellanea--Juvenile literature. I. Armentrout, Patricia, 1960-
 II. Title.
  QL49.A735 2009
  590--dc22
                          2008019696

Printed in the USA

IG/IG

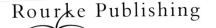

Rourke Publishing

www.rourkepublishing.com – rourke@rourkepublishing.com
Post Office Box 3328, Vero Beach, FL 32964

Table of Contents

Freaky Faces   4

Crocodilian Smiles   6

Fishy Faces   10

Just Jaws   16

Flying Faces   18

Monkey Mugs   20

Creepy Kissers   22

Freaky!!!   24

Tricked Out Muzzles   26

Glossary   31

Index   32

Freaky Faces

Did you know that scientists divide animals into groups? Common features define animal groups. For example, **vertebrates** are a group of animals with backbones. Scientists divide vertebrates into smaller groups as well. Vertebrates include mammals, birds, reptiles, amphibians, and fish.

Can you guess why the elephant seal got its name? It's large snout looks like an elephant's trunk.

Invertebrates are animals without backbones. They include insects, worms, and jellyfish, among others.

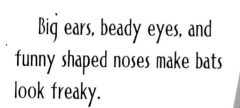

Big ears, beady eyes, and funny shaped noses make bats look freaky.

You can group animals too. Think of things that animals have in common. Maybe they have fur, or four legs, or fins. Can you make a group of animals that all have strange or freaky looking faces? Which ones are in your group?

Crocodilian Smiles

There is something unique about their long pointed snouts, small eyes, and sharp teeth that make crocodile faces freaky. They look **prehistoric**. In fact, scientists think they changed very little since the time of dinosaurs.

Crocodiles will eat just about anything they can catch.

Crocodiles are native to Africa, Asia, Australia, and the Americas.

Crocodiles belong to the reptile order **crocodilian**. Crocodiles are the largest, and one of the most dangerous reptiles. Experts estimate they kill hundreds of people each year.

Alligators kill large prey by pulling them into the water and drowning them.

Alligators are also crocodilians, but they differ from crocodiles. They have rounder snouts and darker skin. Both alligators and crocodiles have plenty of sharp teeth.

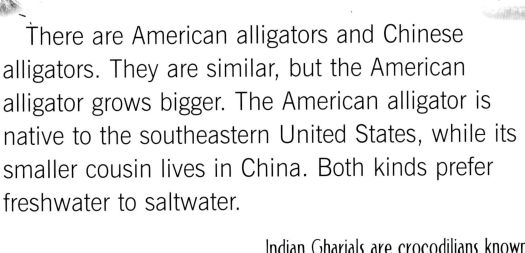

There are American alligators and Chinese alligators. They are similar, but the American alligator grows bigger. The American alligator is native to the southeastern United States, while its smaller cousin lives in China. Both kinds prefer freshwater to saltwater.

Indian Gharials are crocodilians known for their long narrow jaws filled with razor sharp teeth.

9

Fishy Faces

Have you heard of the skinny fish that swims on its side? No, it's not the beginning of a joke. There are actually more than 400 kinds of side swimming fish, known as flatfish. Flounder and halibut are among them. But, if side swimming isn't strange enough, many **species** also have both eyes on the same side of their head!

Flounder, a popular flatfish, eats small fish, worms, and shrimp.

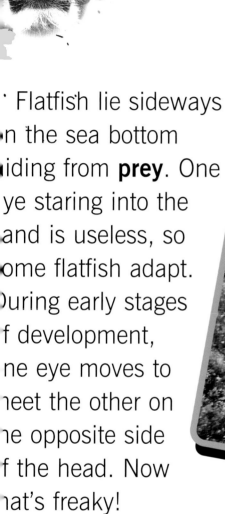

Flatfish lie sideways on the sea bottom hiding from **prey**. One eye staring into the sand is useless, so some flatfish adapt. During early stages of development, one eye moves to meet the other on the opposite side of the head. Now that's freaky!

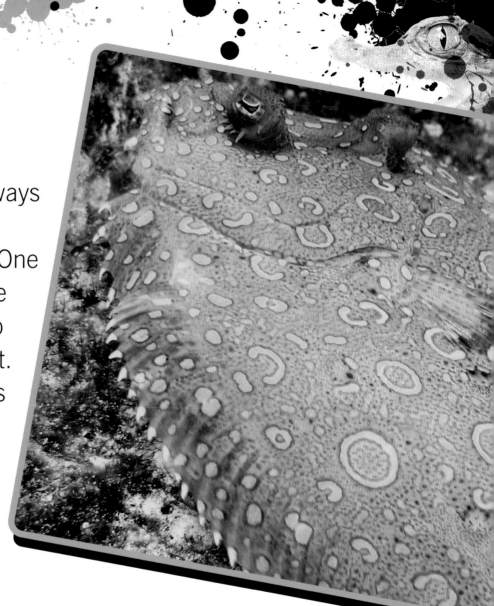

A flounder's coloring helps it blend with its environment.

Flathead fish are not side swimmers, but they have thin bodies and flattened heads. Many species live in the Indian and western Pacific Oceans. Flatheads have eyes on top of their heads and they swim upright. Flatheads are **ambush** hunters. They use **camouflage** to mask themselves in the sand and mud. Then they surprise small fish and shrimp with a quick snatch.

Can you guess why this flathead species is called crocodilefish?

12

Crocodilefish hide in soft sand waiting for prey to swim by them.

The oceans are full of strange looking creatures. Take the sawfish, for instance. Sawfish are rays related to stingrays, skates, and sharks. A sawfish has a long flat snout with teeth. The snout looks like a carpenter's saw. The snout has pores that sense movement. Sawfish use it to find fish, dig for crab, and to fend off **predators**, including sharks.

A sawfish snout is also known as a rostrum.

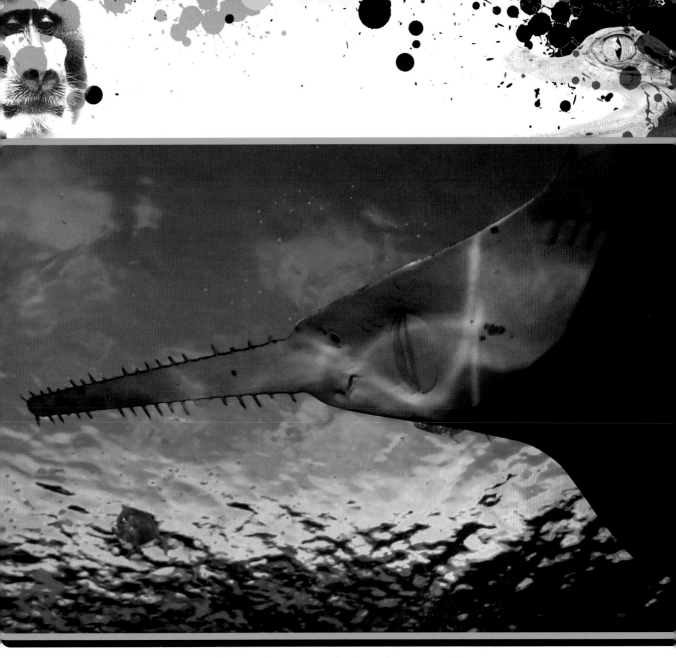

Sawfish slash and wound prey with their long toothy snout.

Just Jaws

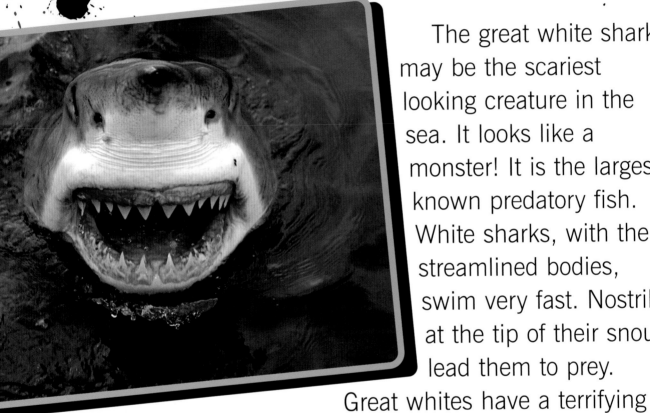

The great white shark may be the scariest looking creature in the sea. It looks like a monster! It is the largest known predatory fish. White sharks, with their streamlined bodies, swim very fast. Nostrils at the tip of their snout lead them to prey.

Great whites have a terrifying set of jaws filled with jagged teeth. Actually, they have rows of sharp teeth. If a tooth is lost in an attack, another one takes its place.

Great white sharks are top predators. They prey on other fish, sea lions, and seals, but eat just about anything they can catch.

The hammerhead shark has a weird head; it is flat and wide. Their nostrils and eyes are set far apart. They look strange but the wide spacing between the eyes and nostrils is a benefit. Hammerheads can easily detect prey by sweeping their head back and forth.

Flying Faces

Some hornbills have a funny looking **casque** on top of their bill. The casque is full of tiny hollow tubes. Why do these birds wear a freaky headdress? Casques vibrate sound. No wonder hornbill calls are so loud.

The Australian pelican has the largest bill of any bird. It uses its bill and pouch like a fishing net to scoop fish from shallow water.

Puffins swim and dive for fish. Did you know puffins sometimes carry dozens of fish at one time in their short, fat, colorful beaks?

19

Monkey Mugs

There are more than 250 kinds of monkeys, and the mandrill is the world's largest. These social **primates** spend most of their day **foraging** in the rainforests of Africa.

Mandrills look like they have painted faces.

20

Mandrills have exotic colorful faces and rumps. Adult males have bright shades of blue, purple, and red on their faces. Excitement enhances the color of the male's rump, which attracts females. Their bright bottoms are also easy for other mandrills in the group to follow as they move through dense, dark forests.

A mandrill displays its large, sharp canine teeth.

21

Creepy Kissers

It is a good thing spiders are so small because you may not want to look at their freaky faces. However, they may be looking at you! That's because most spiders have eight eyes. Spiders also have sharp mouthparts used to grasp food and inject **venom**. One thing they do not have is a set of teeth, so they cannot chew. Instead, they have a feeding tube called a **proboscis**. They use it to suck liquid from their prey, but don't worry; humans are not part of a spider's diet.

Not all spiders have good eyesight. Some can only detect light and movement.

Hunting spiders, such as this wolf spider, use
keen eyesight to hunt and capture prey.

23

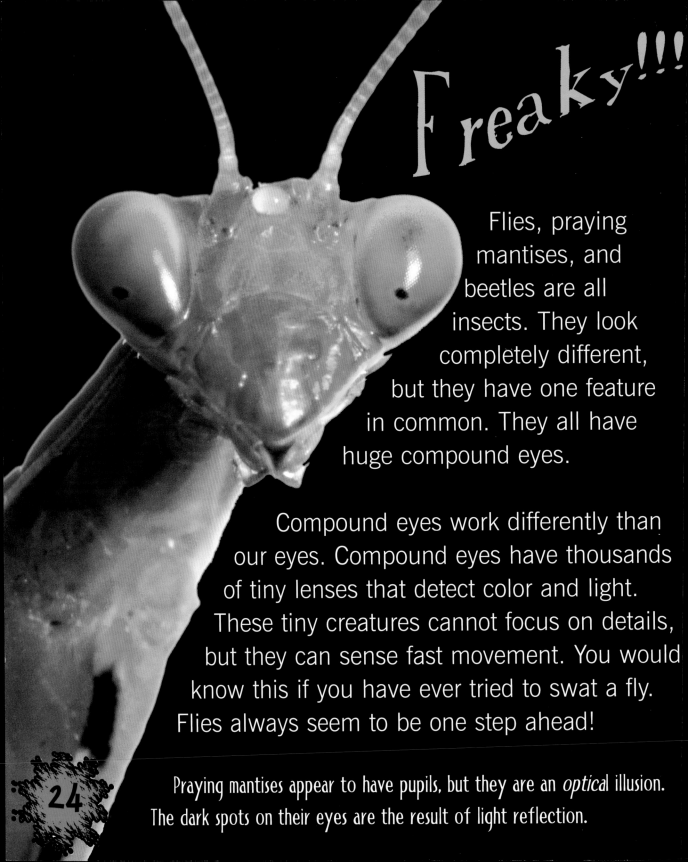

Freaky!!!

Flies, praying mantises, and beetles are all insects. They look completely different, but they have one feature in common. They all have huge compound eyes.

Compound eyes work differently than our eyes. Compound eyes have thousands of tiny lenses that detect color and light. These tiny creatures cannot focus on details, but they can sense fast movement. You would know this if you have ever tried to swat a fly. Flies always seem to be one step ahead!

Praying mantises appear to have pupils, but they are an *optical* illusion. The dark spots on their eyes are the result of light reflection.

The lifespan of an adult housefly ranges from 15 to 60 days.

Some beetles have crushing and grasping mouthparts called mandibles.

Tricked out Muzzles

Most people know the elephant is the largest land animal. Some argue the rhinoceros is the second largest, while others say it is the hippopotamus. All three mammals have unusual faces. The elephant's odd trunk and giant tusks are real working tools. Elephants use their trunks to grasp things. They also use them to suck up water and spray it in their mouth or over their backs. They use their tusks, which are oversized teeth, for digging and scraping.

Both male and female walruses have tusks, which are actually canine teeth.

An elephant has more muscles in its trunk than a person has in their entire body.

Hippos seem to be big and slow, but they are surprisingly fast. They often display the long, razor sharp teeth in their huge mouths when trying to protect their territory.

The rhinoceros looks like an armored tank. Two species, the black and white rhino from Africa, have two horns on their heads. The front horn is larger than the back one. The horns are made of a protein called keratin, the same substance in fingernails and hair. As you might expect, they use their horns to defend themselves and their territory. Males also use their horns when they battle for the affection of females, and couples often butt horns during courtship.

A white rhino's head can weigh almost 1000 pounds (454kg)!

Warthogs look strange with bumpy warts on their heads and our sharp tusks growing from their snout. They use their usks as weapons when threatened by a predator, such as a on or a leopard. Warthogs also use their tusks to dig up oots and bulbs, but they will eat just about anything.

29

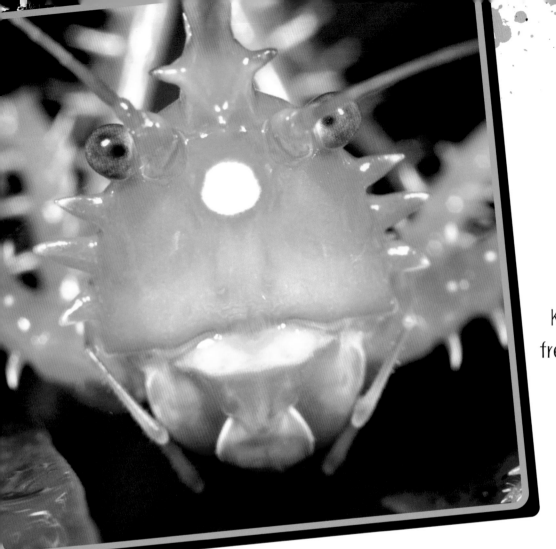

Katydids have freaky faces.

By grouping and studying animals, scientists learn a lot about them. The animal kingdom is full of beautiful, colorful, odd, and strange looking creatures. Some of them may have freaky faces and weird behaviors, but they are all wonderful!

Glossary

ambush (AM-bush): to hide and attack

camouflague (KAM-hu-flahzh): coloring that helps animals blend into their surrounding

casque (KASK): a sometimes brightly colored growth on the top bill of a bird

crocodilian (KROK-uh-DILL-ee-uhn): an order of reptiles that includes alligators, crocodiles, caimans, and gharials, and many forms no longer living

foraging (FOR-ij-ing): searching for food

invertebrates (in-VUR-tuh-brayts): animals without backbones

predators (PRED-uh-turz): animals that hunt other animals for food

prehistoric (pree-hi-STOR-ik): a very long time ago, before written history

prey (PRAY): animals hunted by other animals for food

primates (PRYE-mates): mammals including humans, apes, and monkeys

proboscis (pruh-BAHS-is): an animal's long snout or feeding tube

species (SPEE-sees): one certain kind of animal

venom (VEN-uhm): poison made by some spiders and snakes

vertebrates (VUR-tuh-brayts): animals with backbones

31

Index

alligators   8, 9
crocodile(s)   6, 7, 8
elephant   4, 26, 27
flatfish   10, 11
flathead(s)   12
flounder   10, 11
great white shark   16
hammerhead shark   17
hippopotamus   26, 27
hornbill(s)   18
mandrill(s)   20, 21
pelican(s)   19
puffins   19
rhinoceros   26, 28
sawfish   14, 15
shark(s)   14, 16, 17
spiders   22, 23
warthogs   29

Further Reading

Bailey, Jacqui. *Amazing Animal Facts*. DK Children, 2003.

Hupaperain, Iqbal. *Freaky Facts about Spiders*. Two-Can Publishing, 2007.

Mcghee, Karen. *Encyclopedia of Animals.* National Geographic Children's Books, 2006.

Websites

http://kids.nationalgeographic.com/
http://pbskids.org/krattscreatures/login.shtml?
http://kidsgowild.com/

About the Authors

David and Patricia Armentrout specialize in nonfiction children's books. They enjoy exploring different topics and have written about many subjects, including sports, animals, history, and people. David and Patricia love to spend their free time outdoors with their two boys and dog Max.